CAN I BE FORGIVEN?

CAN I BE FORGIVEN?

In an out-of-the-way cemetery an unmarked tombstone bears the single word, Forgiven. A person can't help wondering, who was forgiven and by whom? What happened that caused someone to leave that message forever engraved upon his tombstone?

The secret of that tombstone has long been buried. But one thing is certain, the need for forgiveness will always exist, since we all fail to live up to our word and others' expectations of us at one time or another.

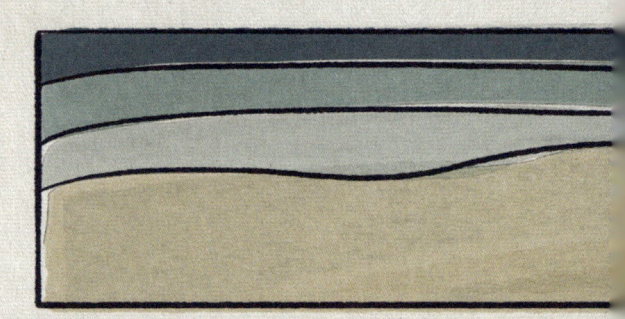

What is more serious is that we have failed to live up to what God expects of us! No one is able to perfectly keep God's commandments. The Bible states it simply, "All have sinned and fall short of the glory of God" (Romans 3:23). "Your iniquities [sins] have made a separation between you and your God" (Isaiah 59:2). Our disobedience separates us from our Creator. We need his forgiveness.

But how can we know that God will forgive us? How could a perfectly just and righteous God overlook our sin? Our situation would be impossible if God had not settled the issue himself. He sent his Son—Jesus Christ—to earth to become a man, live a perfectly sinless life, and ultimately give his life for you and me.

On the cross where Jesus died, he took the punishment for sin that we deserved. The Bible says God made Jesus to be sin for us, the one "who knew no sin, so that in him we might become the righteousness of God" (2 Corinthians 5:21). Then Jesus rose from the tomb and came back to life three days later and was seen by hundreds of people (1 Corinthians 15:3–6).

CAN I BE SURE?

Because of what Jesus has accomplished, it is possible to know that God will forgive you and one day receive you into heaven (John 14:1–3). You can have the assurance of God's forgiveness by making the following choices:

Bible, promises that "to all who did receive him, who believed in his name, he gave the right to become children of God" (John 1:12).

If that is your heart's desire, right where you are you can pray something like this:

Dear God, I know that I have sinned against many people and against you. I need your forgiveness. I believe that Jesus Christ died for me and arose from the dead. I invite him into my life to be my Savior. Thank you for your gift of forgiveness and eternal life.

Are you forgiven?

© 1995 Good News Publishers. Redesign: © 2023. Printed in China.
Bible references: ESV.

CROSSWAY

The Lord Jesus saves all who believe in him.
To learn more about Jesus as Lord and Savior
visit ESV.org/Jesus.